A
MINIATURE HISTORY
OF EUROPEAN ART

A
MINIATURE HISTORY
OF EUROPEAN ART

by

R. H. WILENSKI

M.A.

SECOND EDITION

GEOFFREY CUMBERLEGE
OXFORD UNIVERSITY PRESS
LONDON   NEW YORK   TORONTO

OXFORD UNIVERSITY PRESS
AMEN HOUSE, E.C. 4
LONDON EDINBURGH GLASGOW
NEW YORK TORONTO MELBOURNE
CAPETOWN BOMBAY
GEOFFREY CUMBERLEGE
PUBLISHER TO THE
UNIVERSITY

First edition 1930
Second edition 1945
Second impression 1946
Third impression 1946

PRINTED IN GREAT BRITAIN
7844.4122

PREFACE TO THE 1945 EDITION

IN this Miniature History I restricted myself to one aspect of the story. And when the book first appeared a reviewer in *The Studio* wrote: 'The author traces the influence upon the artist of the Church, the State, the Patron and impersonal forces like the camera and the War. Possibly, the resultant question is, can the artist attain, with any hope of permanence, the condition to which, logically, he must aspire, that of entire freedom to pursue his own ends? Time must answer.' And discussing the final chapter where I referred to the impact of the last war on contemporary art, the same reviewer wrote: 'The war, the author indicates, was the death-blow to the individualist attitude of the artist. He claims that it imposed "the pattern of the age" upon him. The revolt of the artist against the pattern of the age must be written in a chapter which, it is hoped, Mr. Wilenski will witness and record.' I have taken up that challenge in an Epilogue added to this new edition; and I have tried there to indicate that the problem is stated, even if not solved, if the relations between civilization and culture are envisaged in a certain way.

I have also added the new plates XXV–XXVIII illustrating some contributions by culture in the periods discussed in the Epilogue. The pictures shown in the first two have been chosen as original comments on war experience by artists invited to comment by the Ministry of Information; the others, which deal purely with permanent human values, are wholly the outcome of culture's own initiatives.

For the rest I have left the book almost untouched because I stand by the general concept of art history there set down in the 'potted' form required by the scale; and to make a number of changes in detail would be no more than tinkering. Some day, maybe, I shall rewrite the whole thing in a dozen fat volumes as threatened in my original Preface.

LONDON 1945

PREFACE TO THE FIRST EDITION

THE History of Art should, properly, be written backwards, since we all begin by some acquaintance with the art of our own age, and our interest in the art of the past is only a projection of our interest in the art and life that we see around us every day. But such a procedure would involve great technical difficulties in the writing. I have therefore begun this outline history at what we regard to-day as the beginning——the carvings in the caves at Les Eyzies; and I have ended with the Cubist-Classical Renaissance which is still in progress in most civilized lands to-day.

Art historians generally assess the art of the past by their personal aesthetic taste. They select a series of works of art which they like and therefore call 'beautiful' or 'significant in form' and they then tell us that these works are the world's great masterpieces because they contain 'beauty' or 'significant form'. I have not pursued that course in this outline; I have not selected works for mention because I like them nor recorded in any other way my personal taste; I have indulged in no aesthetic criticism; you will find no mention here of the 'rightness of composition' in the work of one artist, or of the 'false notes of form' in the work of another; you will find, I hope, no appreciative or censorious adjectives. In this outline I have set out not to comment but solely to relate.

The ordinary man of average intelligence and average education, who is neither an aesthete nor a philistine, knows that every age has produced a characteristic art; and he has a reasonable curiosity to discover why one age has produced one form of art and another another, and why the age we live in has produced Cubism and not something else.

The first draft of this *Miniature History of European Art* was written in response to a suggestion from the Editor of the *Radio Times* that I should provide him with a 'potted' art history that would, as far as its limits permitted, provide the answer to this curiosity on the part of the average intelligent man. The book has been written in response to a suggestion from the Oxford University Press that I should expand the first draft to the size of a small book.

The work of expansion might of course have been continued till I had written a series of large volumes. But the mounting to a height to survey an age or a century as a whole, which the brevity of this outline has necessitated, has, I believe, brought compensating advantages of its own. Events which had appeared entirely unconnected with the history of art, viewed from this height have appeared as the obvious explanation of a whole wave of artistic production.

Some artists whom we habitually regard as belonging historically to the century in which they lived have been seen as prophets of the art of a century later than their own; while other artists, whom we are accustomed to regard as prominent figures, it has been impossible to perceive at all.

But what appears most clearly from this height is the extent to which the actual *forms* of art have been the result of surrounding circumstances. We are accustomed to regard the history of art as records of certain phases of man's adjustment to his environment. But what we are apt to forget is that the occasions when a generation has *been adjusted* to its environment have been more frequent than the occasions when it has achieved the process for itself. The history of art looked at from sufficient height is seen in fact to be to a large extent the history of the use of artists by powerful individuals or organizations as instruments in the task of imposing some particular form of adjustment upon their generation.

As the centuries advance we see the emergence of a conception of art that makes the artist's function the recording of his personal adjustment to life (or the recording of his failure to achieve one). Rembrandt was the first conspicuous artist who openly made his art a means of personal expression in this way (though there must, of course, have been others,

now unknown, who did the same thing in secret.)
But from my roof-top I perceive that Louis XIV
began the building of Versailles in the year before
Rembrandt died and that Louis XIV was no more
disposed to regard art as the expression of the artist
than a Byzantine Emperor or the Jesuits had been
disposed so to regard it.

In the second half of the nineteenth century, as a
result of the individualism of the age and the romantic movement, the conception of art as the expression
of the individual artist and particularly the expression
of the individual artist's emotional life was so wide-
spread that the average intelligent man put the artist
on a pedestal—and left him there as useless for any
public or material purpose. It was not till the war
produced the Ministry of Information that he was
lifted down again and used.

At the present time the artist (unless he is still
producing nineteenth-century pictures or objects of
mild pleasure for aesthetes or objects to flatter the
philistines' conceit) is in the position of the research
scientist; and his work, which is part of the intellectual activity of the age and a symbol of its pattern,
is exploited by all sorts of people for material ends.

But art is not now being used as an instrument for
enforcing any particular adjustment upon us because
the pretensions of the individualist artists have des-

troyed faith in its collective power. But the power is there; and he would, I think, be a bold man who would tell us that it will never be used again.

I would add that I am well aware that the outline I have drawn is open to the charge of being too materialistic. I know that it presents but one facet of the development surveyed. I know that the perfect art history would be the completion of my outline + an account of the development of man's aesthetic consciousness + an assessment of the relative metaphysical values of art in all its forms. But I doubt if any one living is equipped for such an undertaking. I certainly am not.

HESTON 1930

CONTENTS

CONTENTS

ILLUSTRATIONS

I

PRE-CHRISTIAN ART

1

IF you go to Les Eyzies near Périgueux and climb the side of a mountain you will find an old woman in front of a hole in the rock. The old woman will lead you down a tunnel that seems a quarter of a mile long. You can touch the rock on both sides and above your head; at times the passage grows wider and higher; at others it gets narrower and lower; at one point you have to wriggle, bent double, through a hole. The old woman, holding an electric inspection lamp in her hand, will show you faint carved outlines of bisons on the walls and traces of red-ochre colouring. These bisons, and the similar pictures of bisons and reindeer incised and painted by prehistoric men in other caves and tunnels in the Dordogne and in the north of Spain, are the beginning of art as we know it to-day.

The bisons at Les Eyzies were discovered about sixty-five years ago. At that time they were thought remarkable because they were drawn by torchlight, in the bowels of a mountain, by First-men who probably had no language and who lived, geologists tell us, between 37,000 and 10,000 years ago; but, in England, at any rate, they were not then regarded as 'well' drawn because a vogue for the naturalistic humanized animals of Landseer was then at its height. Nowadays animal drawings much like those in the caves at Les Eyzies are in vogue, and the drawing of these bisons is therefore habitually referred to at the moment as 'amazingly good'.

But these prehistoric drawings and modern drawings of animals are not really comparable things at all. They result from quite different conditions and are therefore quite different in character, though the actual drawing may look much the same. Modern artists draw animals in relative security and comfort; they generally observe the wilder animals in perfect safety at the Zoo. The men who produced the prehistoric pictures lived in a climate which was so cold that half Europe, land and sea, was frozen like the Arctic regions of to-day; they huddled in tunnels in the rock; they had no comfort and no security; they lived in Fear; and their art for that reason had some magic purpose which they thought vital to their existence. We do not know what that purpose was. Perhaps they drew the bisons, reindeer, and other animals to cast a magic spell that might bring luck to their hunting and so mitigate the fear of starvation; perhaps their purpose was something else. We cannot reconstruct the mind of prehistoric man. But we can, I think, be certain that it was not the mind of the modern artist sketching at the Zoo.

2

The oldest civilization, properly so-called, which has left us art, is the Egyptian. It began about five thousand years after the Ice Age—that is, about 3000 B.C., or five thousand years ago. The story of Egyptian art covers three thousand years; it includes the art of the Egypt for which the Jews made bricks without straw, and that of the Egypt of Cleopatra who flirted with Caesar and Anthony.

Throughout the whole of this long period that art remained, relatively speaking, unchanged. Its functions were (*a*) magic—to protect the souls of the dead in their tombs, and (*b*) dynastic—to impress and overawe the populace with the power and majesty of Pharaoh. Hence the pyramids, the largest and most enduring tombs in the world; hence the continuation of the Egyptian convention of drawing in funeral carvings believed to keep away evil spirits from the dead; hence the invention of the most durable design for figure sculpture—the compact figure of solid stone with no projecting arms and legs; hence the imposing, terrifying character of the Egyptians' sculptured portraits of their kings; hence the sphinx, the lion with a human head, which was a symbol of the power of Pharaoh.

The Egyptians also could, and did, sculpt as naturalistically as modern sculptors. But they regarded such work as minor popular art only suitable for statues that had no magic or dynastic function. In the nineteenth century, when European art was naturalistic, the magic and dynastic arts of the Egyptians were regarded as the unsuccessful efforts of men who lived long ago to achieve the naturalistic standards of the Royal Academy and the Paris Salon. Now we know that the forms of Egyptian art were deliberate and devised specifically for magic and dynastic ends.

But there was, nevertheless, one moment in Egyptian history when Egyptian sculpture became individualist romantic art. One Pharaoh was depicted not as Pharaoh the All-Powerful, but as an individual man. He was Amenophis IV, or, as he later called himself, Akhnaton. He brought about a liberal revolution in Egyptian religion, and with it came a moment of liberal Individualism in Egyptian art.

I reproduce his portrait, done about 1370 B.C., now in the Berlin Museum. The nose is broken, but we can see from the mouth and chin how intimately the sculptor has carved the fine profile. We should call this a psychological portrait if it were done to-day; and I cannot resist the temptation of placing next to it a modern psychological portrait—the head known as 'Oriel' by Jacob Epstein.

The Egyptians built vast temples. The hall of the Temple of Karnak, which partially survives, is carried

PLATE I

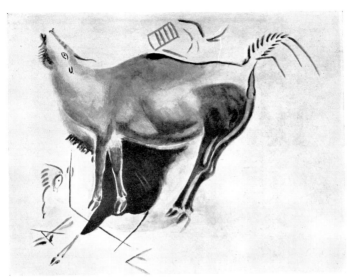

Prehistoric Cave Painting
(*Photo. Giraudon*)

GAUDIER-BRZESKA.   Lioness

PLATE II

Egyptian tomb carving
(*Sakkarah. From* La Sculpture
Egyptienne *by H. Fechheimer,
Cassirer, Berlin*)

Egyptian Sphinx and Pyramid

Assyrian Cherub
(Louvre, Paris)

on a hundred and thirty-seven columns. They invented capitals based on the palm and the lotus. And
they made statues and carvings of a religious character—human figures with beasts' heads, the significance of which we cannot fully apprehend.

3

In the ninth and eighth centuries B.C. an important
dynastic art was produced in Assyria where huge
palaces were built. The vaulted roof, unknown to
the Egyptians, appeared in these palaces; but whether
the Assyrians, or the Persians in the adjacent regions,
invented it, is not established.

In Assyrian art we find the power of the King
symbolized by a winged bull with a man's head—an
equivalent of the Egyptian sphinx. In the Assyrian
language a figure of this kind was called a Cherub
and in Hebrew literature the word Cherubim—('im'
is the Hebrew plural)—was used to denote winged
figures of various kinds. There were Cherubim, we
are told, at the entrance to the Garden of Eden after
the Fall; there were Cherubim in the Tabernacle;
and Hiram of Tyre, the most noted metal-worker of
his age, designed Cherubim for King Solomon's
Temple. The form of these Cherubim was sometimes
based, it would seem from the texts, on the Assyrian
Cherub and sometimes on the Egyptian beast-headed
figures to which wings were added—the Cherubim

described in Ezekiel's Vision, for example, have the heads of a man, a lion, an ox, and an eagle. Later the terrifying Assyro-Egyptian-Hebrew winged man-beast becomes the Greek 'Nike' or 'Victory', later still the Christian winged man or Angel, and finally it becomes the little naked child with butterfly wings that we now call a 'cherub'.[1]

The Assyrians appear to have invented the carved narrative frieze; and the interiors of their palaces were decorated with such friezes narrating the King's exploits in war and in the chase; representations of slaughter and torture of men in war and slaughter of animals in the chase especially appealed to the Assyrian monarchs.

The famous bas-relief called the 'Lion Hunt' in the British Museum, which was made about 800 B.C., is characteristic of this art. The sculptor could draw with great naturalism, and did so when occupied with the wounded lions—a part of his subject which the King wished to see portrayed as naturalistically as possible. But when the artist came to the portrayal of the King he had to make him a Fear-inspiring figure, and he portrayed him accordingly in a stiff attitude and used a strictly formal non-naturalistic style. Thus it comes that in one and the same panel

[1] By another progression the Egyptian sphinx which in original monumental examples still fills us with awe became eventually the ormolu mounts on the Louis XV furniture designed for the boudoirs of the King's favourites.

we have what appears to our eyes the strangest differences in technique.

4

While the Babylonian artist was carving the 'Lion Hunt', Homer was welding the folk-lore of the Greek Archipelago and the Aegean into the epic poems that told of the Trojan War fought two hundred years before. Homer wrote at a time when the Greeks were recovering from the destruction of Aegean civilization by northern Greek barbarians about 1000 B.C. Of the civilization then destroyed, which had begun about the same time as the Egyptian civilization, no works of functional, i.e. magic or dynastic, art remain. But excavations have produced a few gold cups and other relics which show that, like the Egyptians and the Assyrians, the ancient Greeks used naturalistic drawing in their minor works.

Greek art, as we understand it, begins about the time of the death of Homer. For three hundred years, from about 750 B.C., the forms of Greek art were derived from the art of the Egyptians. Then from about 550 B.C. Greek work assumed the special character which has exercised so great an influence on art.

Greek art from the middle of the fifth century onwards represents the first escape of the major arts

from Fear. The Egyptians and Assyrians, as noted,
had a naturalistic art for minor works, and the kings
and priests allowed the minor artists freedom in such
work. But they allowed no such freedom to first-rate
artists whom they employed for magic and dynastic
ends. The Greeks also had a naturalistic art for
minor works; but in Greece both the minor artists
and the first-rate artists were granted liberty of mind.
No priests dictated traditional forms of magic art to
the great Greek artists; no shadow of an all-powerful
king oppressed them. Classical art, i.e. the conscious
creation of finite formal harmony and unity for its
own sake, was invented in Greece because there was
no tyrant in Greece to employ artists to terrify his
subjects and because there was nothing in the Greek
religion to prevent the artists working out proportions for their own sake when building a temple or
making a statue of a god.

The Greek temple, of which the Parthenon is the
type, was a development of the Egyptian. But it was
always on a smaller scale; there is no attempt in
Greek art to impress by sheer size and bulk. The
Greek artist was concerned with adjustment of proportions and with delicacy of execution in the decora-
tion. The celebrated Doric, Ionic, and Corinthian
columns were developments of the Egyptian columns;
and from the Assyrians the Greek artists took the
notion of the narrative sculptured frieze.

Greek sculptors produced narrative friezes for temples, and Cult Images of gods and goddesses. The Greek religion called upon its artists to represent gods and goddesses as 'ideal' men and women. The artists' attention was therefore directed to the study of the human form for this purpose, and the Greeks were the first to develop the conception of the 'ideal' human nude. The Greek sculptors also made Social Images in honour of national achievements and popular personalities—politicians, men of letters, athletes, and so forth.

Pheidias who directed the work on the Parthenon, Myron (who worked before and after 450 B.C. and was the author of the Discobolos), Praxiteles, and Lysippus are among the Greek sculptors whose works have to some extent survived.

Greek potters made objects of daily use and took trouble with the architectural problem of their form. They decorated them with conventional patterns and narrative drawings of subjects connected with religion and legend, and sometimes with 'genre' scenes connected with the function of the vessel.

In the later periods the best known potters made pots that were intended not for use but purely for ornament. This progression from a functional to a purely aesthetic purpose is one that often occurs in many aspects of art. A form devised for a special service is afterwards repeated and developed for its own sake though the service for which it was called into being is no longer demanded of it—just as in life a custom often survives and is cultivated for its own sake long after its purpose has become obsolete or has been forgotten.

The Greek painters were employed at times to enhance the decorative effect of architecture and sculpture; at other times they were employed to colour the sculptured friezes in the temples in order that the subjects might be recognizable at a distance, and to colour the statues to make them look more 'natural'.

We know the names of two or three Greek painters who were much esteemed in their day. But no pictures or frescoes survive.

5

Alexander the Great died in 323 B.C. He had taken his armies from Macedonia to India and founded a new centre of Hellenic culture at Alexandria. But he had left Italy alone; and in Etruria, in Central Italy, there was a civilization that was closely in touch with the minor arts of Greece across the water. Etruria had escaped Alexander; it was not, however, to escape the Romans who were next door and about to start on their career of conquest. Rome conquered Etruria about 280 B.C. and from that time till—at the beginning of the Christian era—the Roman republic became an Empire, with a God-Emperor, Roman art was mainly a blend of Etruscan and Greek art applied to Roman funerary and religious purposes.

Imperial Rome's contribution was building. The Romans built temples, aqueducts, arenas, and triumphal arches. They built them wherever they went for the service of their armies of occupation and to impress the subject peoples with the power and dignity of Rome. They built their temples on Greek models; in their other structures they adopted the Perso-Assyrian vault and developed the round arch. The Romans built so stoutly that we can see their work to-day in Italy, in Provence, and many other places; and we see imitations of it everywhere— witness the Arc de Triomphe at the head of the Champs Elysées in Paris and the Marble Arch at the north-east entrance of Hyde Park.

Roman sculptors copied and imitated Greek religious images. But they were mainly employed in the construction of imposing images of the God-Emperors and their wives, which were set up in public places, and in carving reliefs, narrating the military exploits of Caesar, on the triumphal arches and on commemorative columns. They were also called upon to make 'idealized' images of the Emperor's favourites, and to manufacture portrait busts of court personalities, national heroes, and rich people who sat to them in the same spirit that rich people sit to painters and sculptors to-day. No Roman painting, except a few portraits, and some hack decorations in Pompeian villas, survives.

Roman art was thus a development of the Egyptian and Assyrian conceptions of art. The Roman artists were not free as the Greeks had been. They had to serve the dynastic, imperial, and social purposes of Rome. But the influence of the free-minded art of Greece acted unceasingly on Roman production; and though in spirit the Romans reverted to dynastic Fear-inspiring art, their production was never purely Fear-inspiring in its form.

PLATE III

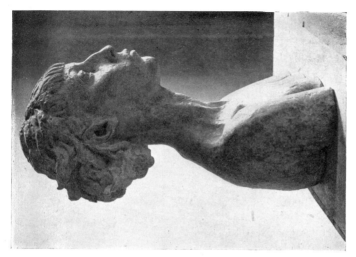

EPSTEIN
Oriel
(Photo. Paul Laib)

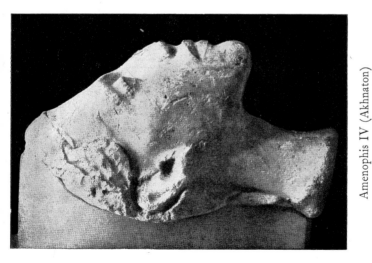

Amenophis IV (Akhnaton)
(Kaiser Friedrich Museum, Berlin. From La Sculpture
Egyptienne by H. Fechheimer, Cassirer, Berlin)

PLATE IV

PRAXITELES
Hermes (detail)
(*Photo. Alinari*)

II

MEDIEVAL CHRISTIAN ART

I

THE term 'Medieval Christian Art' means the art produced in Christendom from the beginning of the era to the end of the fourteenth century. The Medieval period thus covers a span of time that is more than twice as long as the span between the beginning of the Renaissance and the present day; and in that long span Christian art was born, became enslaved, and was finally set free.

At the beginning of the fourth century the Emperor Constantine realized that Rome was not geographically well-situated as the capital of the vast Roman Empire, and he built Byzantium (thereafter known as Constantinople) to be the capital of the Eastern regions while Rome remained the capital of the West.

This double Roman Empire contained the civilization of Rome, the civilization of the Jews (which admitted no graven image of their God), and the civilization of Alexandria. All three civilizations had their influence on Christian art.

The earliest Christian monuments, the Catacombs in Rome—the subterranean tombs where the early Christians buried their dead—were decorated with

paintings in the style used in the Pompeian villas of
the Romans, because many of the painters were
converted Romans accustomed to paint in that way.
But the early Christians also included large numbers
of converted Jews, who had not forgotten the old
prohibition against the graven image, and for that
reason, and perhaps also on grounds of prudence, the
Catacomb painters drew no figures of God or Christ,
such as occur soon afterwards in Christian art, but
drew instead Orpheus, whom the faithful accepted
as a secret symbol for Christ, Daniel in the Lions'
Den, in which they recognized the Resurrection,
and so forth.

The Emperor Theodosius made Christianity the
official religion of the Empire in 388. From that
date the organized Church began to establish and
direct a Christian art. With its revenues from the
faithful, and supported by Imperial wealth and
Imperial power, it now built churches all over the
Empire, and at the same time it spread the Gospel by
means of illuminated manuscripts which made clear
the narratives of missionaries to people who could
not read.

The celebrated church of S. Sophia (now a
mosque) in Constantinople, was inaugurated by the
Emperor Justinian, as Head of the Church, on
Christmas Eve in 537. The interior was covered all
over with mosaic pictures in gold and a thousand

colours (like the interior of St. Mark's in Venice, which was copied from it six hundred and fifty years later); and Christian art for the first thousand years consisted of mosaics on church walls or drawings in manuscripts. This art was influenced by traditions from the East and by the traditions of Alexandria—the city which, founded by Alexander the Great and bequeathed to the Romans in 80 B.C., was the intellectual centre of the Empire for three hundred years.

On these foundations Byzantine art developed in its own way, and soon assumed a character that was nearer to that of Egyptian magic and dynastic art than to that of the free and gentle Christian art that was to be developed in the late Middle Ages. The Emperor in Constantinople was all-powerful, like a Pharaoh. Though a Christian he still felt himself Caesar, the God-Emperor, and he demanded worship; and at the same time he was head of the Christian Church, above both the Byzantine and the Roman pontiffs. The Christian Church at this period was the slave of the Byzantine Emperor; and the art which it established was enslaved to the same master who regarded it as a means of impressing the people with the holy might of Caesar and the sanctity of the holy Church.

Under the dual direction of Caesar and the Church Byzantine art depicted the sacred figures in Christian history in rigid, fear-inspiring images intended to mirror the denizens of Heaven conceived on the model of the Byzantine Imperial Court. At one moment the Church even countenanced images of haloed Caesars in churches. In Ravenna, in the Church of S. Vitale, you can see mosaics of the Emperor Justinian and his wife, Theodora, who both have haloes round their heads, and elsewhere in Byzantine mosaics and manuscripts there are images of haloed Emperors above whose heads attendant angels hold their crowns.

But the Church was not to remain for ever in Byzantine fetters. The Pontiffs in Rome grew steadily in power till in 730 the Pope felt strong enough to defy the Emperor Leo the Isaurian and to defy him on this very point of images. But oddly enough it was the Emperor (influenced perhaps by Mohammedan taunts against the 'idolatrous' Christians) who forbade the use of images and ordered their destruction throughout the Empire, and it was the Pope who insisted on their retention; and Christendom witnessed the astonishing spectacle of the Pope declaring war against the Byzantine Caesar on behalf of a form of art which the Byzantine Caesars had originally imposed upon the Church. This war was actually fought; the Byzantine troops were defeated, and the Emperor was excommunicated. It was the only time that a war has been fought about art.

PLATE V

The Empress Theodora

(From the mosaic group in the Church of S. Vitale, Ravenna)

(Photo. Anderson)

PLATE VI

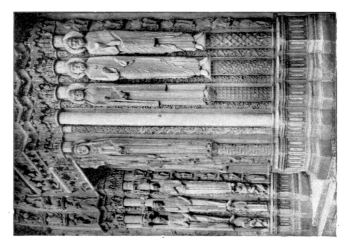

The Old Porch
(*Chartres Cathedral. Photo, Houvet*)

April and July
(*Chartres Cathedral. Photo, Houvet*)

As one result of this Iconoclastic war the Pope's position was consolidated, and by 800 the Pope and the Emperor Charlemagne combined to found a new Holy Roman Empire in the West from which Byzantine authority was finally excluded.

Another result of this was was the continuation of the Byzantine forms in European art for a further two hundred years. The Church had defended and now retained the rigid Fear-inspiring Byzantine images and the fixed formulae for the sacred scenes in the narrative manuscripts, because the faithful had learned to venerate the images and to regard the style and the formulae as exclusively appropriate for religious art; and the Greek Church in Russia, for this reason, has retained the Byzantine style in its eikons almost to the present time.

But a change came after the year 1000, which Christendom expected to be the end of the world. When the year passed a cloud lifted and Western Christendom, with surging enthusiasm, began to build churches and cathedrals and to invent for the purpose a whole series of new forms of art.

2

This wave of confidence and enthusiasm continued for three hundred years. The churches that arose in the eleventh century in the Franco-German regions of the Holy Roman Empire were built in the style known as Romanesque, which corresponds to the Norman style in England. We can still see this style at Cahors, Conques, Arles, and many other places in France, and at Durham, St. Albans, Chichester, Ely, Winchester, and other places in England. Then at the beginning of the twelfth century the French invented the Gothic cathedral; and all over France, the Netherlands, Germany, and England large edifices with pointed arches, soaring pillars, vaulted roofs, and lofty towers, and a wealth of sculpture and stained glass were erected.

The Gothic cathedrals were built by the people and for the people. The entire population of whole regions were employed for generations on their construction; they were the work of hundreds of designing artists and thousands of executing craftsmen; and they expressed the knowledge, the faith, and the spirit of the later Middle Ages which tried to reconcile St. Dominic's heretic-hunting conception of religion (which had its roots in Byzantine tyranny) and the gentler conception associated with St. Francis.

In the Gothic cathedrals we have the old tradition of Byzantine Fear-inspiring formalism in continual conflict with new, free, and gentler forms. At Chartres, the most characteristic of all Gothic cathedrals, we have carved figures in the Byzantine style round the oldest porch, and figures of rigid saints in one set of windows; but the rose windows were designed by men who had regained the Greek freedom of mind and who were allowed to create in line and colour for their own sakes; and in other windows, given to the Cathedral by the various trade guilds, we have pictures of members of the guilds, weaving, tanning, and so forth, and selling their wares to customers. Moreover, side by side with the sculptured figures in the old rigid styles there are carved figures symbolizing the months and seasons by peasants engaged in seasonable work. Thus 'April' examines the blossom of his fruit trees to see if it has 'set', and 'July' cuts down the corn.

The presence of this 'genre' art in the Gothic cathedrals speaks a spirit quite different from that of the haloed Emperor and Empress at Ravenna. It speaks the spirit that was expressed elsewhere in the sermon of St. Francis to the birds, a spirit that was to grow and find still further expression in art through the life and work of St. Francis himself.

St. Francis died in 1226; and his official life by St. Bonaventura was commissioned in 1260. The Franciscan Legend, with its series of tender and dramatic episodes, made a wide popular appeal. Giotto painted the life of St. Francis in the Franciscan Church at Assisi at the very beginning of the four-teenth century; he painted it again in Florence and other places; and all through the century it was a favourite subject with the Italian painters who evolved for it a new narrative art that was free, tender, and dramatic. This Franciscan narrative art was of supreme importance, because it opened the path for free, tender, and dramatic pictures of the life of Christ—for such pictures, in fact, as Giotto himself painted on the walls of the Arena Chapel in Padua, where we can see them to this day.

Giotto worked not in mosaic but in fresco, i.e. in tempera colours direct on the plastered wall; and this art of fresco painting was used from the beginning of the fourteenth century to the end of the fifteenth and, later still, for mural pictures in thousands of churches in Italian towns.

Compared with oil painting, which was not used till later, tempera painting on walls or panels demands great precision of the artist, because the colours dry at once, and it is almost impossible to make alterations; but compared with the working of mosaic, the process is relatively free, because the artist can move the brush rapidly and achieve the most delicate curves. Thus the painters who were now allowed by the Church to tell the sacred stories with individual touches had also the freedom of a new technique to help them in their task.

Fresco painting was a specifically Italian development made possible by the accident that the Gothic style in architecture, which sacrificed wall space to

PLATE VII

DUCCIO
Virgin and Child
(*Private Collection. Photo. Anderson*)

PLATE VIII

GIOTTO
The Angel visiting St. Anne
(*Arena Chapel, Padua. Photo. Anderson*)

stained glass, was not taken up with great enthusiasm in Italy where the architects preferred to develop the Romanesque traditions which provided ample wall-space for this Gothic narrative art.

3

In addition to their mural frescoes the fourteenth-century Italian artists painted altar-pieces for churches and private chapels. These pictures were in tempera on wooden panels and they were fixed in elaborately carved, gilded, and jewelled frames.

These works consisted generally of a centre panel depicting the Virgin and Child or the Annunciation, and panels depicting the patron saints of the region were often placed on either side. Under the altar-piece there was often an oblong panel called a 'predella' in which the Passion or the life of a saint was narrated.

In the narrative predellas as in the narrative frescoes the artists often produced what seem to us quaint and childlike illustrations. But to the spectator of this later medieval period the pictures did not seem at all childlike and quaint. To the medieval mind these pictures were as awful and piteous as the most awful and piteous Tintoretto or Ribera is to us. In front of brightly coloured little illustrations of the martyrdom or miracles of Christian saints the medieval spectator thrilled with horror or ecstasy because he regarded the pictures as literal records of divinely inspired fact.

In one predella of this period we see the dead body of St. Bernardino being carried through the streets, and as the corpse passes a sinful woman the holy contact drives the devil from her; and the artist has represented this by painting a little black devil coming out of her mouth. To the medieval spectator this was a plain statement of what actually happened, and he reacted emotionally to the happening in a way that is impossible to the modern spectator.

In other cases we tend to react emotionally to the subjects portrayed in these predella pictures when the medieval spectator would certainly have been unmoved. There is a predella which shows the burning of a goldsmith, his wife, and children, because the goldsmith had inadvertently received a silver pyx stolen by a woman from a church. To the modern mind the savagery of such justice is appalling. But the medieval mind contemplated such an execution and its presentation without horror because every one in the Middle Ages had no doubt that good spirits and devils actually inhabited human frames, and when the Church burned and tortured those who denied or questioned religious doctrine or those who, like the goldsmith, were guilty of sacrilege, every one regarded the torture as a charity to the victim because it drove the devil from his body and set free his soul from the devil's grasp. In the case of the goldsmith it was obvious to the medieval mind that the whole family were inhabited by devils and that the flames alone could compass their release.

In these predellas, when ordinary people were shown taking part in the episodes, the artists made full use of their new freedom to look at nature and record their observations, and their technique here, as in the narrative frescoes, is relatively speaking realistic. But in the Virgin and Child panels the artists retained the formal silhouette and gestures of the Byzantine tradition, because their aim was to dehumanize the sacred figures and present them as divine—since the representation of the Virgin and Child as a real mortal woman and a real mortal child would have appeared to them a gross impiety. But even in these formal figures these artists suffused the Byzantine tradition with the new spirit and with gentle observation.

With these painters of the late Middle Ages we arrive at the period when artists signed their names to their pictures. The dictated art of Byzantium had been anonymous because the artists were treated as tools by their employers. The art of the Gothic cathedrals was also anonymous—because every one contributed to it in some manner or degree. The artists of the fourteenth century signed their names because they were the first Christian artists who were expected to furnish individual work.

The most famous artists of this time worked in Siena and Florence. The Sienese names are Duccio, the Lorenzetti, and Simone Martini; the Florentine names are Giotto, Lorenzo Monaco, and Fra Angelico who lived right through the early fifteenth century— the period of transition between the Middle Ages and the Renaissance.

III
RENAISSANCE ART

I

IN the fifteenth century Italy was covered with small, nominally republican city-states, ruled by one or more rich or noble families, who all had miniature courts which were continually parading for military and hunting expeditions, in wedding processions, carnival celebrations, and so forth. Artists were employed at these courts; they designed the pageantry, and drew from it, in return, the material not only for pictures of contemporary processions, but also for pictures of the Adoration of the Magi, where the Kings eventually became portraits of local notabilities followed by their courts.

Thus, in the Medici Palace in Florence, we can see the 'Journey of the Magi' painted all round a private chapel by Benozzo Gozzoli; the Kings are members of the Medici family, and the procession really represents a hunting expedition from the Medici Court; and in Santa Maria Novella, in Florence, we can see Ghirlandaio's frescoes of 'The Birth of the Virgin' and 'The Visitation', where ladies of the Tornabuoni family with their attendants are shown as spectators of the sacred scenes.

Thus also the painter Piero di Cosimo was widely

famous as a designer of carnival celebrations; Uccello's celebrated battle picture, now in the National Gallery, was one of four panels painted for a Medici bedroom; the banner carried by Giuliano dei Medici in a famous tournament was designed by Botticelli; and Leonardo da Vinci, employed at the Sforza Court of Milan as engineer and pageant master, designed costumes and processions, and a bath for the Duchess Beatrice in the castle park.

2

Italian pageantry of the fifteenth century was accompanied, on the one hand, by numerous local wars and, on the other, by the revival of learning and rediscovery of antique art that are known as the Renaissance.

The wars had little effect on the character of the art produced or on the lives of the artists. They were fought in the main by Condottieri, or professional captains of arms, who sold their services and those of their soldiers to any Duke or ruling body ready to pay for them for purposes of ambition or of greed. When battle-pictures were painted at this period they were conceived as pageant-scenes or tournaments. No Renaissance artists have left us burning protests against war's horrors such as later centuries produced, because the Renaissance wars were less horrible than later wars and on a much smaller scale.

But the revival of learning, known as Humanism, and the rediscovery of the antique had very considerable effects on art, and these effects increased all through the second half of this century and beyond the first quarter of the next.

3

To the end of the fourteenth century men had looked to the Church for their knowledge as well as for their faith. Now men had reached a stage when secular studies were established in their own right. Mathematics and chemistry, geography and history, were now objects of independent study; and the introduction of printing contributed to a movement which included the study of Greek and Latin literary works.

The Renaissance Church still demanded service from the artists and employed them to paint altarpieces and frescoes in churches, monasteries, and convents, and to carve figures and bas-reliefs. But the service now demanded was the most learned, the most skilful work which the artists could produce. The Church, as it were, impounded the new secular science on principle, though for the Church's purposes the science was of no particular use.

It is important to realize that this Renaissance religious art was not really religious art properly so-called, because the form of the works was evolved not for a religious purpose but as a demonstration of the artist's technical powers; and this is why Ruskin attacked the Renaissance masters who, he wrote, 'polluted their art with the science of the sepulchre, and degraded it with presumptuous and paltry technical skill'.

The scientific movement of the Renaissance extended to all fields of art. In architecture it involved the study of ancient Greek and Roman monuments and the creation of a new Renaissance-classical style; and in sculpture and painting it led the artists to intensive study of all kinds of technical problems—anatomy, perspective, composition, and so forth.

4

Each region produced its own demonstrations of this Humanist skill. Padua, for example, a University town, produced a characteristically learned art. It had a famous Art Academy directed by one Squarcione, a keen collector of Graeco-Roman statues and reliefs. Squarcione made his pupils draw from these antiques and he gave them a tremendous grilling in anatomy and perspective. Both Cosimo Tura and Mantegna were pupils in his school, and Giovanni Bellini of Venice also worked there at one time. Mantegna was the chief demonstrator of Paduan science. The

PLATE IX

GOZZOLI

Procession of the Magi (detail)

(*Medici-Riccardi Palace, Florence. Photo. Anderson*)

PLATE X

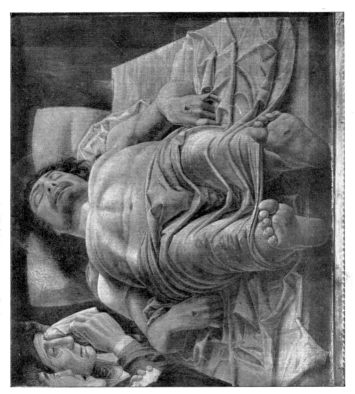

MANTEGNA. Dead Christ

(*Brera, Milan. Photo. Anderson*)

complicated perspective in his frescoes in the Eremitani Church was widely famous; and there is foreshortening in his 'Dead Christ' which the Church would never have permitted in the Middle ages.

5

Then in Milan there was a school of Humanist artists who were pupils or followers of Leonardo da Vinci. Like the Paduan artists they frequently painted their figures not from life but from antique sculpture.

Leonardo himself had a truly scientific mind. He was architect, engineer, research scientist, sculptor, and painter. He had an intense curiosity to discover the organic nature of phenomena; and the knowledge at which he arrived in many fields was the wonder of his contemporaries and is still the wonder of his biographers to-day.

Leonardo grasped the inner architecture of ancient Greek sculpture and his painting was a translation of that architecture into the newly discovered medium of oil paint. The head of 'St. Anne' in the picture of 'The Virgin and St. Anne' in the Louvre is such a translation of the head of the Hermes of Praxiteles. All Leonardo's heads have this character; and if a head ascribed to him has any other character we can be certain that the attribution is wrong.

6

In the region of Rome the new science produced a demonstration of anatomical knowledge by Luca Signorelli in large mural paintings for the Cathedral of Orvieto, and compositions turned out by Perugino and Pintoricchio who were in partnership as a firm of ecclesiastical decorators and who at one time had Raphael as an apprentice on their staff.

7

When we turn to Florence we find another aspect of the Renaissance,—a Neo-pagan art produced by the patronage of a cultured clique.

Florence had her own scientific Humanist painters, men like Masaccio, whose paintings in the Carmine Church were a technical inspiration to several generations of Florentine artists, and Pollaiuolo, who is said to have been the first painter to dissect corpses in his anatomical studies. But Florence also had the wealthy Medicis as art patrons and in the Medici circle culture was very much 'the thing'.

A sense of the past, an interest in the ancient pagan world, and an appreciation of the examples of Graeco-Roman sculpture that were continually being unearthed, were essential characteristics of any aspirant to the Medici circle, which collected antique sculpture, read the Greek and Latin poets and commissioned Neo-pagan Latin verse from Humanist poets and Neo-pagan pictures from the painters.

The art produced in these conditions was purely private in its character. The people as a whole had taken part in the public art of the Gothic cathedrals. But in this private art of the Renaissance the people had no share. Renaissance art was an aristocratic art produced by cultivated artists and enjoyed by a cultivated ruling minority of the population. The people as a whole saw the scientific Humanist art of the Renaissance which was painted for churches. But they knew and saw nothing of the Neo-pagan Hedonist art produced for private mansions in Florence and villas just outside it. Had the people seen this art, with its nude and lightly draped figures, it would have appeared to them a rather suspect diversion of the rich, just as, I imagine, the Russian Ballet must have appeared to, say, London taxi-cab drivers or the miners of South Wales, and as this Florentine art appeared to Savonarola who called on the people to burn it in the public square.

Botticelli was the outstanding Neo-pagan Hedonist painter of this Florentine clique. His 'Birth of Venus' and 'Spring' were painted for the country villa of young Lorenzo di Pier Francesco dei Medici, who had inherited a fortune from his banker father and spent it on entertaining Neo-pagan poets and painters and producing 'high-brow' amateur theatricals, while his cousin Lorenzo the Magnificent was engaged in politics and more public patronage of art. Both pictures are illustrations to verses by the Neopagan poet Poliziano, who was a great favourite at the Medici Courts; and in both Botticelli has based the figures on antique sculpture. His 'Venus' is a translation of the antique 'Medici Venus', the dancing figures in his 'Spring' come from some antique of 'The Graces', and the figure of Mercury in that picture is a translation of the antique statue known as 'The Satyr' by Praxiteles.[1]

8

In Venice the pageant art of the early Renaissance had been developed in characteristic forms. The Venetians had always been proud of their lovely city which in the fifteenth and sixteenth centuries took on the appearance which we know to-day. Venetian pageantry and processions were famous even in the pageant age, and Venice was not only the centre of an empire but also a pleasure city for the world. Venetian pageantry was recorded by Gentile Bellini,

[1] The so-called 'Spring' should properly be entitled 'The Court of Love'. It illustrates an episode in a poem by Poliziano which celebrated the feats of arms and loves of Giuliano dei Medici and contained a scene in the Garden of the Queen of Love where the Graces, Spring, Flora, and the Zephyrs are in attendance. The picture may be a record of an amateur performance of this poem in ballet or dramatic form in Lorenzo's villa, as the head of Mercury is traditionally supposed to be a portrait of Giuliano.

PLATE XI

LEONARDO DA VINCI
Virgin and Child with St. Anne (detail) (cf. Pl. IV)
(*Louvre, Paris. Photo. Alinari*)

PLATE XII

RAPHAEL
Parnassus
(Vatican, Rome. Photo. Anderson)

Carpaccio, and other painters, and thanks to their records we know exactly what happened when the whole of Venice turned out to watch a procession in the square before St. Mark's.

In the sixteenth century the Venetian painters developed these local traditions in large and sumptuous decorative pictures in which Humanist science and Neo-pagan motifs were incorporated; and the pictures of Titian and Veronese are the expression of Venetian opulence and splendour, of Venetian power, and of Venetian religion, which was closely dovetailed with the service of the State.

But between Venetian pageant art of the fifteenth and Venetian decorative art of the sixteenth century there stands the figure of Giorgione. This artist produced a new form of Neo-paganism for the ladies in Venetian palaces and in the villas on the mainland. His art was the equivalent of the art produced by Botticelli for the dilettanti of Florence; and it was painted at almost the same time.

9

In the later years of the fifteenth century and the first quarter of the sixteenth the Vatican became infected with Neo-pagan culture. The Popes and Cardinals began to form private art collections of their own with galleries of antique sculpture and cabinets of gems; and they soon surpassed the Medicis as personal patrons of the arts.

The Renaissance Popes believed that they had thus evolved a perfect combination of Humanism and Theology. They felt themselves exceedingly broadminded in thus accepting Renaissance Neopaganism in art and Renaissance Hedonism in life and believed that this attitude could be reconciled with the execution of the Church's functions and the maintenance of the Vatican's power.

This illusion was about to be shattered by the Reformation and ghastly religious strife; but the Renaissance Popes were able to hug it with satisfaction for a brief period, and it lasted long enough for Raphael to record it in his frescoes in the Vatican.

Raphael's frescoes in the Camera della Segnatura, so called because it was here that the Popes affixed their seals to documents, depict the elements of this Papal compromise for which the world at that time was so far from ripe. On the right wall of the Stanza Raphael painted Theology or 'The Church Triumphant' (known erroneously as 'The Dispute of the Sacrament'); on the left wall he painted Philosophy or 'The School of Athens' where the philosophers and geometricians of antiquity are portrayed; and on the other walls he painted Poetry or 'Parnassus' where Apollo and the Muses with the poets of Greece and Rome are grouped on Parnassus, and

'Law' typified by pictures of the Emperor Justinian and Pope Gregory XI dispensing articles of faith.

These pictures which thus express a particular attitude to life were planned and carried out as architectural designs. For Raphael was essentially an architect. He made the first plan and model for the new St. Peter's; he built the Loggia of Leo X in the Vatican; and he was Director of Excavations of Ancient Roman Monuments and made plans for the restoration of the buildings that he unearthed.

It is important to remember the architectural nature of Raphael's main achievements because the popularity of certain of his portraits and of his easel pictures for churches (most of which were painted by his pupils from his rough designs) has obscured the true character of his life's work.

10

In the Western lands there was no scientific Humanist or Neo-pagan Renaissance comparable with the Italian. Gothic art, which was indigenous in the West and had produced such imposing monuments, was too firmly rooted in France and the Netherlands for the influence of the Italian Renaissance-classical movement to affect it in more than superficial ways.

Francois I invited Leonardo and other Italian artists to his court and their influence is seen in the French painting of the School of Fontainebleau; and

there are Renaissance elements in the fundamentally
Gothic chateaux which the French nobles erected on
the Loire. But French art really remained Gothic
all through the fifteenth century.

In the Netherlands Italian Renaissance influences
are seen in the pictures of Quentin Matsys and others,
but Flemish painting was essentially Gothic from the
Eycks to Pieter Brueghel.

In Spain the Renaissance-classical innovations are
hardly perceptible at all. Spain had been enriched
with the buildings put up by the Moors, and this
influence is seen in Spanish Gothic architecture and
also in such buildings as affected to some extent the
Italian style; and in painting Spain passed almost
directly from imitations of Flemish Gothic pictures
to the Spanish contributions to the art we call
Baroque.

When the sixteenth century dawned conditions
outside Italy were mainly too troubled and too grim
for a new scientific-Humanist or Hedonist art to
develop. While the Renaissance-classical buildings
were being built in Rome, Florence, and Venice,
and Raphael was calmly painting in the Camera
della Segnatura, Torquemada was robbing, burning,
strangling, and tearing out tongues in Spain; before
Raphael died, Martin Luther had burnt the famous
Papal Bull in Wittenberg; and while the Venetians
were painting their care-free decorations, Alva and

PLATE XIII

MICHELANGELO
The Last Judgement
(*Sistine Chapel, Rome. Photo. Anderson*)

PLATE XIV

RIBERA

St. Sebastian

(Trado, Madrid. Photo. Anderson)

Titelmann were robbing, burning, strangling, and tearing out tongues in the Netherlands; and it was not till the struggle with Spain was over that Rubens appeared to speak the language of the Venetian decorators with a rich Flemish accent that was all its own.

IV

SEVENTEENTH-CENTURY ART

I

THE seventeenth century produced (*a*) the Baroque art of Italy and Spain, (*b*) a Picturesque-classical school in Rome, (*c*) the Protestant art of Holland, and (*d*) 'Society' portraits.

Baroque art was an accompaniment of the Counter-Reformation of the Jesuits who blamed the Renaissance popes for having allowed art, especially painting and sculpture, to become a means of satisfaction to the private patron, and for having neglected its power as a propaganda arm of the Church Militant. The Jesuits, in an effort to make up for what they regarded as serious backsliding, built hundreds of new churches in which they employed hundreds of artists to paint altar-pieces and ceilings.

The altar-pieces thus commissioned were to depict scenes of martyrdom on earth, painted in a way that would move the spectator to pity and terror in the highest degree; the ceilings were to display scenes of ecstasy in Heaven painted in a way calculated to excite the spectator to religious exaltation.

The artists were called upon, in fact, to supply a form of art that would have its effect by its own dramatic intensity or its own sentimental appeal; a form of art that would have on the troubled mind of the seventeenth-century spectator the same result as the art of the Middle Ages had achieved on spectators of that time.

In this task the artists were helped by the work of three earlier masters, Michelangelo, Tintoretto, and El Greco, who had all worked in the sixteenth century and developed art in just the direction which the Jesuits now desired for their campaign.

Michelangelo had seen that the compromise so dearly believed in by the Renaissance popes and Raphael was a tragic illusion. He had sensed the movements of unrest and the rising passions of his own age and the next; and he knew that neither the science nor the Hedonism of his time would stand up against the coming storm. He painted Sibylls and Prophets in the Sistine Chapel; and he was himself a prophet, unheeded, of the tragedy to come. In contrast with the calm confidence of Raphael's work in the Vatican the art created by Michelangelo was the passionate thunder of a harassed mind. Raphael's work praised an 'ideal' ordered and static world. Michelangelo's lamented a world of confusion and a rush of war.

Michelangelo's work in Rome had been continued in Venice by Tintoretto, the *terribilita* of whose achievements had impressed spectators in his day: and Tintoretto's work had been continued by El

Greco who was trained in Venice and then went to live in Spain.

The Baroque artists of the Counter-Reformation adapted the qualities of these original Baroque masters to the Jesuit purpose, and converted the thunder and compassion of Michelangelo, Tintoretto, and El Greco, to the rant of the tragic actor and the leading lady's tears.

Nevertheless this theatrical Baroque art, with its violent gestures, crude horrors, forced sentiment, and dramatic light and shade was the last form of religious art properly so called that has yet appeared. The Baroque movement was the last attempt of the Church to create new forms of religious art. Since then the Church has been content with artistic *pastiches*, and religious art has become the expression of the individual artist's personal religious faith.

Caravaggio, Domenichino, Guido Reni, and Ribera were among the Baroque painters in Italy. Murillo was a characteristic figure in Spain.

The Baroque artists also painted non-religious pictures for private patrons, and these pictures exhibit the characteristic Baroque technique. But we must not forget in examining the Baroque secular pictures that the dramatic light and shade and the imposing naturalism which characterize them had been invented for the Jesuit religious purpose, and are only incidental in such works as Caravaggio's 'Narcissus' in Rome, or Guido Reni's 'Atalanta's Race' in Naples.

2

In the seventeenth century Rome occupied the position in the art-world that Paris occupies to-day. Artists and students of all nationalities went there to study the arts, and the foreign colony in Rome produced its own development of art.

This development can best be described as the invention of the picturesque-classical furniture picture for the houses of the rich. In the construction of such pictures the artists obeyed the classical principles of Renaissance composition. Some painted pagan subjects; others evolved the Classical-picturesque landscape based on the backgrounds in the works of the Renaissance masters, notably Carpaccio.

The outstanding painters of this development were two Frenchmen both domiciled for the greater part of their lives in Rome—Nicholas Poussin and Claude Lorrain.

3

Meanwhile, another form of art was being developed by the Protestants in Holland. The Dutch after the social revolution which followed the fight with Spain soon became prosperous and soon produced a confident middle class. The Dutch middle-class man of moderate means called for pictures that would flatter his vanity, for pictures describing a world in which he could feel at home, and above all for pictures that he could afford to buy. In response to this demand there arose the Dutch portrait, the Dutch 'genre' picture, and the Dutch landscape, which depicted the Dutch middle-class man, his wife and family, his home and his favourite dog, the meadows where his cattle grazed, the taverns where he met his friends, the hovels where his labourers lived, the sea that was the source of his prosperity, and the food and drink in which he copiously indulged.

These pictures proved a huge success. The demand became great, and the supply—since small naturalistic pictures of this kind are quite easy to paint—soon outdistanced the demand. Holland in the seventeenth century produced thousands of painters, and hundreds of thousands of pictures, most of which were bought in the open market, like boots or vegetables, and for prices that were much the same.

At the same time there was a Renaissance in Holland. 'Culture' became the fashion among the merchant princes of Holland as it had been the fashion among the merchant and ecclesiastical princes in Florence and Rome; and side by side with the popular art for the middle classes there was a Humanist Dutch-Italian art produced for a cultured minority by Dutch artists who had worked in the foreign colony in Rome or who were influenced by Italian painting of the time.

The names of the Dutch artists of the two classes are too numerous to detail (the curious may find some in the book I have devoted to this school[1]), but one Dutch artist stands apart from all the others—Rembrandt—the creator of Individualist art.

With Rembrandt we have, in fact, a new art, an art describing the artist as a man. Some people like Rembrandt's manner of painting; others find it messy and dull; but no one denies that in Rembrandt's work we have contact with an artist who was translating his personal thought and feelings into paint. And this is equally true whether the subject is a portrait or a religious theme; for while the Italian and Spanish Baroque painters were making the last important effort to achieve official religious art, Rembrandt was creating a new type of religious picture—the picture expressing the artist's personal religious faith.

Rembrandt is the founder of the Romantic movement of the nineteenth century which mistrusted all art that served a public purpose and proclaimed the doctrine that the only art of value was art which expressed the artist's personal reactions as an individual man.

[1] *An Introduction to Dutch Art*, by R. H. Wilenski (Faber & Faber).

4

Social conditions in all countries in the seventeenth century favoured the production of the 'Society' portrait. In Renaissance times most of the painters, including the masters—Raphael, Titian, Tintoretto, and Rubens, for example—had painted such portraits on their off-days; and a few painters had specialized in this type of work. In the seventeenth century the number of the professional 'Society' portrait painters very much increased; and some of the painters became exceedingly rich men.

Santvoort and Van der Helst were the most successful 'Society' portrait painters in Holland. Van Dyck had great success in Antwerp, Genoa, and England; and Velasquez was the 'Society' portrait painter of the Court of Spain.

PLATE XV

FUMIANI. Ceiling (detail)

(*Church of San. Pantaleone, Venice. Photo. Alinari*)

PLATE XVI

REMBRANDT
Christ Carried to the Tomb
(*Etching. British Museum*)

V

EIGHTEENTH-CENTURY ART

I

IN the year before Rembrandt died Louis XIV began the rebuilding of Versailles, and inaugurated a new era of dynastic art that rivalled the dynastic arts of the Pharaohs in Egypt and of the God-Emperors of Rome.

Louis XIV was 'the Lieutenant of God'. He took the sun as his emblem; he was the Roi-Soleil; and he built the Palace of Versailles as his temple. More than half the nobility of France was domiciled in this vast palace and engaged continuously in ceremonious ritual round the person of the King. The Royal establishment numbered fourteen thousand persons; five hundred men were employed on the ceremonies connected with the King's meals; a hundred nobles carried out elaborate ceremonies when he arose in the morning; as many more attended when he retired at night; and when courtiers passed through his chamber—whether he was present or not—they genuflected before the Royal bed as before an altar in a church.

The whole artistic resources of France were concentrated in glorification of Louis XIV at Versailles and in Paris. Versailles Palace with its Hall of Mirrors, its gilt and painted ceilings, its carved woodwork and sumptuous furniture, and Versailles Park with its endless vistas, its lakes and gardens, are still with us—though a little dilapidated—as the prime symbol of this last dynastic decorative art that was imitated in all the palaces of Europe for a hundred and fifty years. In the heart of Paris we can still see the Place des Conquêtes (now called the Place Vendôme and the home of dressmakers) that was built to honour the Roi-Soleil, and in Paris also we can see the Porte St. Denis and the Porte St. Martin, the Roman triumphal arches that were put up to welcome Louis, the new Caesar, after victories in Germany and Holland.

A vast French industry of applied art was created for Versailles by the Roi-Soleil's minister, Colbert, the Mussolini of his time, who worked sixteen hours a day and reorganized France. Colbert encouraged the Gobelins, Aubusson, and Beauvais makers of fine tapestries, he founded the Sèvres factory to compete with German porcelain, the St. Gobain factory to compete with Venetian glass, and the Alençon lace factory to compete with English and Venetian lace. His aim was to acquire for the French the reputation of the finest artist-craftsmen in Europe, because he knew that such a reputation would be a great cash asset to the State. He succeeded; the reputation and the revenue persist to this day.

In pursuance of the same policy Colbert organized the French Academy of Fine Art in Paris; and in Rome he founded a branch of the French Academy as a central meeting place for the colony of French artists and students.

Louis XIV died in 1715. Louis XV continued the decorations of Versailles, and both Madame de Pompadour and Madame du Barry were keen patrons of the decorative arts. But the Court was no longer the sole point of focus for the French architects, sculptors, painters, tapestry and cabinet-makers, porcelain manufacturers, and so forth. Paris now contained a large number of cultivated private patrons among the aristocracy and upper bourgeoisie, who employed artists and craftsmen right up to the Revolution. There was also a large demand from abroad for pictures and furniture by the French eighteenth-century artists. All the palaces and great houses built in imitation of Versailles required furniture in appropriate style; and on the eve of the Revolution—which temporarily destroyed the whole industry—France was exporting work by her artist-craftsmen to an annual value of 3,000,000 livres.

The character of French decorative art throughout the eighteenth century can be studied in the Wallace Collection at Hertford House. There we can see the sometimes classical and sometimes flamboyant, and always admirably made furniture, the Sèvres por-

celain, the bronzes by Falconet, and the marble portraits by Houdon; and there, in painting, we have
the boudoir pictures of Watteau and his followers,
the rococo decorations by Boucher, arbiter of taste
in the reign of Louis XV, the light fantasies of
Fragonard who lived right through the Revolution,
and the work of Chardin who translated into French
terms the Dutch pictures of domestic life.

2

Meanwhile there were artistic developments in
England. While Hardouin-Mansart was building
Versailles, Sir Christopher Wren was rebuilding
St. Paul's, and the buildings put up by Wren at
Hampton Court were an imitation of Hardouin-
Mansart's style. At the same time, the West End
of London was rebuilt in the Dutch red-brick style
that we can still see in the Temple, Queen Anne's
Gate, Barton Street, and elsewhere—the style that
continued through the first quarter of the eighteenth
century, and was determined, in so far as materials
and proportions were concerned, by an Act of Parliament after the Great Fire.

The second quarter of the eighteenth century
marks the beginning of English painting properly
so called—for while Boucher was painting in pink
and blue the Rising and the Setting Sun (that hang
on the stairs at Hertford House) as designs for

PLATE XVII

RIGAUD
Louis XIV
(*Louvre, Paris. Photo. Bulloz*)

PLATE XVIII

GAINSBOROUGH.   Mrs. Moody and her Children
(Dulwich Gallery. Photo. W. F. Mansell)

tapestries that were to delight La Pompadour, Hogarth was painting the 'Marriage à la Mode' series (that we can see in the Tate Gallery) and making his drawings for 'Beer Street' and 'Gin Lane'.

Hogarth had to live by the sale of engravings from his satirical pictures, because in the reigns of the first two Georges the English moneyed aristocracy adorned their houses with foreign pictures, mostly old masters, bought in Italy on the 'grand tours' that were then considered an essential part of the education of fashionable young men. For the same reason Richard Wilson, who painted Classical-picturesque landscapes in the style of Claude Lorrain, was unable to sell his pictures for the greater part of his life though English collectors had been among Claude's most enthusiastic patrons.

But by the time George III had been king ten years the situation was different. By 1770 portraits by English painters had become fashionable, and in the applied art also there was a demand for English work.

The change was brought about by the great increase in English wealth and political power in the mid-eighteenth century. Wealth creates the desire for elegant surroundings. Robert Adam, who could design elegant houses, was therefore called on to build Syon at Brentford, Osterley a few miles away, Ken Wood at Hampstead, the Adelphi on the river, and so forth; Wyatt, Chambers, Dance, Holland, and Soane were called upon for other mansions; and Nash built the Regent Street Quadrant and terraces in Regent's Park.

Elegant surroundings call for elegant appointments; and this demand by the rich men of the eighteenth century called forth the elegant furniture of Chippendale and his successors, the silver work of Sheffield designed to harmonize with the Adam and Chippendale styles, and the porcelain of Worcester, Derby, and Chelsea.

The English craftsmen of the eighteenth century were all excellent workmen, quite as excellent as their colleagues in France, and for their designs they looked frequently to the same source of inspiration, i.e. the Graeco-Roman art of the excavations round Naples which Mme de Pompadour's architect brother had been among the first to copy and adapt. But, unlike the French, they were able to continue their work to the end of the century and into the first decades of the next. Then, when the machine age came, this English craftsmanship perished, though we all still use machine-made copies of this art to-day.

It was the fashion all through the eighteenth century for English travellers to bring back antique Graeco-Roman marbles from their Italian grand tours, and mansions like Holkham and Petworth contained notable collections. Towards the end of the century this taste was at its height and one Gavin Hamilton, an English painter who had turned dealer, was able to sell scores of antique marbles from the Villa d'Este, and Hadrian's Villa at Tivoli, and other places, to Lord Shelbourne and other collectors in England.

This fashion and the influence of the Italian sculptor, Canova, led the English sculptors of the late eighteenth and the early nineteenth century to assume that the function of sculpture was to imitate the works of ancient Athens, Alexandria, and Rome.

Great possessions produce self-satisfaction, and self-satisfaction produces a demand for portraits; and just as the wealthy Dutch in the seventeenth century found Van der Helst and Santvoort, so the wealthy English in the eighteenth found Gainsborough and Reynolds.

Gainsbrough took Van Dyck as his model. He could catch a likeness, and he made the ladies who sat to him appear extremely thin. Reynolds tried to combine the techniques of Rembrandt and Titian. He made the ladies who sat to him appear more healthy than those of Gainsborough. But he had great difficulty about the likenesses, and many of his portraits were refused by the sitters because the resemblance was not considered good.

With the increase of the prestige of art and artists in England it became the fashion for young ladies to learn drawing and painting. The demand created a supply of drawing masters. One of these, John Crome, a drawing master of Norwich, who imitated the landscapes of the Dutch painters, was the leader of the group of similar painters known as the Norwich School; and Norwich-Dutch landscapes, with rather brighter greens, were painted at the turn of the century by John Constable.

3

Art in Venice in the eighteenth century also developed in characteristic forms. Venice in this period was more than ever the pleasure resort of Europe. Carnival, when masks were worn, lasted for six months in the year, from the beginning of October to Christmas, and from Twelfth Night to Easter, with an additional fortnight for Ascension. Life in Venice was now one round of gaiety. The patrician families shirked the offices of State and spent all their time in the arms of women or at the gambling establishments of which the city was then full.

In this atmosphere the Venetian painters of the eighteenth century produced views of Venice and other places with the aid of a camera obscura, little journalistic pictures of Venetian carnival and social life modelled on the Dutch pictures of the preceding age, and decorations for the palaces of such patrician families as were still disposed to spend their money in this way.

PLATE XIX

GÉRARD. Eros and Psyche
(*Louvre, Paris. Photo. Alinari*)

DELACROIX. Liberty Leading the People
(*Louvre, Paris. Photo. Giraudon*)

PLATE XX

WIERTZ
Nineteenth Century Civilization
(*Wiertz Museum, Brussels*)

GOYA.   Disasters of War
(*Etching.   British Museum*)

The principal view-makers and social chroniclers were Canaletto, Guardi, Bellotto, and Longhi. The principal decorator was Tiepolo who imitated Veronese and adapted the technique of the Baroque ceiling painters to secular subjects, using the effects of perspective devised by the Baroque religious painters to suggest the flight of sacred figures through the roof to Heaven, for the purpose of suggesting the flight of Venus and pink Cupids above the heads of dancers and gamblers at the Ridottos.

4

In the reign of Louis XV the French Academy of Art started an annual Salon, or public exhibition of its members' works; these Salons have continued in France to the present time, and similar exhibitions now take place in most European capitals. The Paris Salons and other such exhibitions created a one-day-a-year-art-inspecting public whose taste soon began to influence art, because artists began to work with a view to producing sensational or journalistic pictures to attract attention from this public. Such exhibitions, moreover, soon created the art-critic, because the one-day-a-year-art-inspecting public demanded guidance in finding its way round, and men who made the study of pictures their profession came forward to act the part of guides.

In England the Royal Academy of Art was

founded in 1768 and Reynolds was elected the first President. Reynolds worked incessantly to improve the status of the artist in this country. He instituted the Academy banquet to which royalty, the aristocracy, and high personages of State were invited; and he worked hard himself to make and hold a position in the social world. His work has proved successful; sixteen members of the Academy to-day are knights.

Both the French and English Academies established art schools which provided training in accordance with the artistic standards that prevailed among the members at the time.

VI

NINETEENTH-CENTURY ART

I

THE French Revolutionary Government made the painter Louis David its art-dictator. David had been trained in the French Academy in Rome. As art-dictator he designed and organized Revolutionary *fêtes* and processions and abolished the Academy and the artist-craftsmen's guilds. Art under David's direction was restricted to Revolutionary propaganda, either direct, as in his own picture of the 'Death of Marat' in Brussels, or indirect, as in austere pictures of classical subjects, in which the supposed virtues of Republican Rome were intended to symbolize the virtues of the new Republic. Under David's rule it was more than a man's life was worth to produce decorative art in the light style of the old régime. Boilly, an engraver of dainty *scènes galantes*, was denounced to the Revolutionary Committee, and only saved his head by hastily beginning a large picture of a Revolutionary subject.

Napoleon, First Consul in 1800, Emperor in 1804, found time between his campaigns to call for a new dynastic art to celebrate his triumphs. He summoned David to paint the vast picture of his coronation, now in the Louvre, and the picture

called 'The Emperor distributing Eagles', now at
Versailles; he re-established the Academy, and re-
vived the cabinet-making industry by demanding a
new 'Empire' style to decorate his palaces and those
of Josephine and Marie Louise. But his reign was
too short and harassed to permit of a new dynastic
art comparable to that of Louis XIV. He ordered
the Arc de Triomphe at the head of the Champs
Elysées in 1806 to celebrate the victories of La
Grande Armée, and he made alterations in the architect's design with his own hand, but he was not
destined to witness its completion, and only his ashes
brought back from St. Helena passed beneath it.

The Napoleonic wars called forth a number of
characteristic pictures. Gros, who had fought in
Napoleon's battles, painted the episode at Jaffa
(when Napoleon, to encourage the morale of his
troops, made a personal inspection of soldiers suffer-
ing from fever in the hospital), and 'Napoleon at
Eylau', where from a pile of dead and dying a
wounded soldier rises on his elbow to cry, 'Vive
l'Empereur!' as Napoleon passes.

On the other hand, Goya, stirred to the depths of
his being by the horrors of the French invasion of
Spain, paused in his regular work of painting portraits and produced a set of etchings of war in all its
brutality that are among the tragic documents in art;
and Wiertz in Brussels painted 'Napoleon in Hell',

and the picture called 'Nineteenth-Century Civilization', which shows a woman leaping from a window
with her child in her arms while soldiers fire at her.

2

After the fall of Napoleon the annual Salons became
the central point of focus of French art; the general
public became patrons, and Louis XVIII, Charles X,
Louis Philippe, Napoleon III, and the Republican
Governments became merely individual patrons in
that public. At the same time the artists began to
quarrel among themselves about the principles that
should govern their production. The attack on the
decorative art of the late eighteenth century, made
as Revolutionary propaganda by David, had set a
precedent for attacks on David's own art-principles
as soon as those principles had ceased to have a
propaganda value and had to stand on their own legs;
and all through the century there was a continuous
battle between the apostles of 'classical' art based on
ideas of order, and the apostles of a new aesthetic of
individual expression—an aesthetic called the Romantic movement—which was an aspect of the
Individualism that came out of the French Revolution.

Both sides in this battle carried formidable guns,
because both sides were artistically well educated.
The Revolutionary Government had sequestered
works of art and also the great Royal collections, and

had transferred them to the Louvre, which had become a national museum open to the public. Napoleon, moreover, had looted works of art in Italy, and the Louvre galleries were crowded with Italian old masters which the Parisian art students could study until 1815 when the Allies returned them to Italy. Both groups of artists were thus able to point to precedents for their art principles. The Classicists pointed to Graeco-Roman art and Raphael, and the Romantics to Gothic freedom, the passion and movement in the works of Michelangelo and Tintoretto, and the individualism of Rembrandt. The Classicists drew strength from the ensconced position of their Academy stronghold, while the Romantics had behind them the driving power of the mental outlook of the time which mistrusted ensconced authority and formal order, and put its faith in unfettered individual endeavour.

Leading painters of Davidian 'classical' pictures were Gérard, Girodet, and Ingres—though Ingres was a Romantic at heart.

Leading Romantics were Géricault and Delacroix.

3

The demonstration of these rival principles took the form of huge pictures painted for the Paris Salons, where the public, though they imperfectly comprehended the principles, expressed preferences for one type of picture or the other, in much the same way that the public nowadays express preferences at Brooklands, though they imperfectly comprehend the rival principles of construction that are being demonstrated by the cars.

As these demonstration pictures had not been demanded by any religious, political, or social organization, the problem of what to do with them when the Salon closed became each year more embarrassing. Like the 'Blue Bird' or the 'Golden Arrow', the pictures were of no use to any section of the public, but it seemed a pity to destroy them. The Luxembourg Palace was accordingly arranged as a Gallery to receive them, and other galleries were established in the French provinces to take some of the overflow.

4

Meanwhile, the once-a-year-art-inspecting public that went to the Salons, a public consisting for the most part of the prosperous middle class that had grown up since the Revolution, were demanding small pictures for their homes and demanding, as the Dutch middle classes had demanded before, that these pictures should be portraits of themselves, their surroundings, and their daily life; and hundreds of painters replied by painting such pictures in imitation of the Dutch pictures of two centuries before.

5

Then in the middle of the century the camera arrived. This event had no effect on the painters of the Salon demonstration pictures which had become by this time mainly demonstrations of the artists' desire to attract attention in the show; and it had no effect on the painters of pictures of everyday life for middle-class homes. But by thinking artists it could not be ignored, and in the second half of the century there arose a new type of artist—the artist consciously engaged in the quasi-scientific activity of attempting either (*a*) to rival the camera, or (*b*) to discover exactly what the painter can achieve that is denied to the intelligent man armed with a camera, and to build up a new art of painting based on this residuum. Nineteenth-century Romantic art in its culminating form, Impressionism and Post-Impressionism followed as results of this quasi-scientific activity.

Nineteenth-century French Romantic art in its culminating form was a continuation of the Individualism of Rembrandt. The artists extracted from Rembrandt's art the element of personal comment that could not be achieved by the camera and built their own art on that. They sought unusual emotive fragments in the world around them and stressed the unusual and emotive aspects of those fragments in

PLATE XXI

RENOIR
Box at the Theatre
(*Courtauld Collection, London. Photo. Bulloz*)

PLATE XXII

FRITH. Derby Day (detail)

(National Gallery, London. Photo. W. F. Mansell)

their work. This art was essentially the expression of the individual artist's emotional reactions. It set out to serve no public purpose. It was personal emotional comment for its own sake.

Outstanding figures in this experiment were Degas, Van Gogh, and the sculptor Rodin.

The French Impressionists tried to defeat the camera at its own game. They realized that the camera could only record degrees of light, obstructions to light, reflections of light, and relations of light and shade; and they experimented in the quasi-scientific activity of recording phenomena as the camera records them but with the addition of colour. They limited their palette to the colours of the spectrum, and recording everyday life around (as the descriptive painters of pictures for French bourgeois homes were doing and as the Dutch painters had done before), they limited their records to effects of phenomena in spectrum-coloured light.

Outstanding figures of this experiment were Monet, Renoir, Sisley, and Pissarro.

The Impressionists, intent on the quasi-scientific study of the play of coloured light, abandoned as unnecessary for their purpose the particular aspects of scientific skill which had come into art in the Renaissance and Baroque times—the knowledge of anatomy, perspective, dramatic composition and so forth. They were soon joined by painters who found that this freedom from the Renaissance and Baroque standards revealed the possibility of a new and enchanting pastime—the rapid notation in oil paint of transitory effects. Thrilled with this discovery these painters launched a new conception of the painter's function. 'Oil painting', they cried in delight, 'can defeat the camera when it is oil painting for oil painting's sake'.

The outstanding artist of this calibre was Manet.

The Post-Impressionists who were transitional figures between nineteenth- and twentieth-century art continued the slow fighting retreat before the camera's onslaught. They called for a revival of the principles of formal decorative composition which the Impressionists had rejected and they experimented with devices based on the composition in Oriental art which was then being studied for the first time in France.

The outstanding figure in this experiment was Gauguin who went to the South Sea Islands in a desperate attempt to find inspiration in fresh material.

6

There was at first no public to buy the work of these artists who were fighting for pictorial art against the camera. Manet at the age of forty had not sold a picture; and both Van Gogh and Gauguin lived in poverty till they died. The derivative painters of the

Salons who buried their heads in the sand and denied the camera's menace declared that the 'new-fangled' painting was merely eccentricity and incompetence; and the general public were likewise blind to the real situation.

But, gradually, thinking critics and dilettanti began to see what these several forms of effort were about; appreciation of the experimental pictures grew; and gradually dealers came forward to invest in the works at low prices, to put them in storage, and to sell them eventually with handsome profits for themselves.

7

In England the most striking feature of the first half of the century was the artists' ignorance of the art productions of the past. A few artists travelled abroad but the majority remained at home and were almost entirely unacquainted with the works of the Old Masters. There were magnificent old pictures and many antique marbles in the private mansions of the wealthy; but the ordinary artist never saw them; and the names of most of the Old Masters were mere names to the English art-student till the Prince Consort arranged the historical art displays in the Crystal Palace and in the Art Treasures Exhibition in Manchester, and Ruskin's influence encouraged gifts to the National Gallery, which was built in 1838, but did not contain a representative collectiontill the later years of the century.

The annual exhibitions of the Academy (like the French Salons) were now the centre of focus for English artists, and to attract attention in these shows soon became an indispensable condition of success.

The Academy, true to the ideal set by Reynolds, made these exhibitions primarily social functions where portraits of well-known people were displayed; but it also hung (*a*) illustrations to Shakespeare and other pictures to intrigue or impress the general public, and (*b*) the concoctions of Turner who was a globe trotter and alternated between the picturesque-classical furniture-picture tradition of Claude, the new Romantic creed that he had come across in Paris, and the Norwich-Dutch naturalism of Constable, and (*c*) small rural landscapes and descriptive pictures of everyday life on the Dutch and Franco-Dutch models which the general public could buy for their homes.

8

Then, in the year 1848, two or three young art students looking through a book of engravings of frescoes by a fifteenth-century Florentine vowed to imbue their pictures with the Pre-Renaissance spirit as they conceived it; and at the same time these 'Pre-Raphaelites', as they called themselves, set out

PLATE XXIII

PAUL NASH.   We are making a New World

(*Photo. by Imperial War Museum, London*)

PLATE XXIV

Modern American Buildings
(*Photograph by Hoppé*)

to defeat the camera by attempting to rival its un-selecting vision and by 'going', as Ruskin exhorted them, 'to nature, rejecting nothing, selecting no-thing, and scorning nothing'.

Outstanding figures in the Pre-Raphaelite experi-ment were Millais and Holman Hunt.

The opposite attempt to defeat the camera—the attempt to limit painting to functions outside the camera's powers—was made here by Whistler, an American, who had studied in Paris and was acquainted with the works of the Impressionists and of Manet.

The effect of the Pre-Raphaelites' work in the 'fifties and that of Whistler in the 'seventies is well known.

'Hideous', 'revolting', 'disgusting', 'deformed', 'loathsome', 'absurd', 'affected', 'ill-drawn', and 'puerile' were some of the adjectives used of the Pre-Raphaelites' pictures; *The Times* accused the artists of disorder of mind and eye, and declared that 'this morbid infatuation which sacrifices truth, beauty, and genuine feeling to mere eccentricity . . . deserves no quarter at the hands of the public'; the *Athenaeum* said: 'Their ambition is an unhealthy thirst which seeks notoriety by means of mere conceit. . . . Their trick is to defy the principle of beauty;' and a clergy-man published a pamphlet beginning: 'Woe, woe, woe to the . . . young men of stubborn instincts calling themselves Pre-Raphaelites.'

Whistler was regarded by the Academic artists as an impostor and Ruskin accused him of 'flinging a pot of paint in the public's face'.

9

While the Pre-Raphaelites and Whistler were being reviled, Frith was making a fortune from subject pictures of everyday life which were exhibited in the Academy (where a policeman was stationed to keep back the crowd) and afterwards engraved; other painters were doing the same thing; yet others were imitating the Paris Salon demonstration pictures and attracting attention in the Academy that way.

As the English demonstration pictures, like their French prototypes, had not been called for by any religious, political, or social organization, and as, like their French prototypes, they were frequently of enormous size, the same problem of what to do with them after the Academy exhibition also arose here; and eventually the Tate Gallery and galleries in provincial cities were instituted to receive them.

10

The influence of the French Romantic movement, which exalted the Gothic above the Renaissance-classical tradition in architecture, caused a Gothic revival here from the second quarter of the century onwards. The Houses of Parliament were completed in 1850 and the Law Courts in 1882. Ruskins's writings about Gothic architecture contributed to the spread of this movement, which was reflected in the applied arts. William Morris, who wove pseudo-Gothic tapestries with his own hand, inspired the Arts and Crafts Movement which tried to revive hand industry to combat the advance of machine-made furniture, pottery, and so forth. The influence of the Pre-Raphaelite movement also contributed to a Gothic revival, as far as subjects were concerned, in the paintings by Pre-Raphaelites of the second generation.

Burne-Jones, who combined imitation of the pictures by Botticelli with a pseudo-Gothic Pre-Raphaelitism, was a Pre-Raphaelite of the second generation.

When the century closed the general public were admiring works by Burne-Jones, by the imitators of Whistler, and by Watts who painted pictorial sermons in a technique imitating the sumptuous decorative art of the Renaissance Venetians.

VII

TWENTIETH-CENTURY ART

I

IN the bird's-eye review of the centuries that have preceded our own we have seen important religious and social organizations demanding art for religious and social purposes, dictating the character of that art, and paying the artists for their pains; we have in a word seen such organizations calling the tune and paying the piper. But in the nineteenth century we have observed that no such important religious or social art-employing organizations existed; that in their stead there had arisen new organizations consisting, in France, of the Academy of Art, the Salon Jury, and the Beaux Arts Schools, and, in England, of the Royal Academy, the Academy Jury, and the Academy Schools; and that the purpose for which these organizations had arisen was understood to be not religious or social but artistic.

This position continued in both countries in the fourteen years that preceded the first world-war; and the 'artistic' Academic organizations had by this time become so powerful (not only in France and England but in most other countries as well) that they assumed the right to dictate the character of the art of the age, though they were not able to employ artists in any

PLATE XXV

STANLEY SPENCER
Shipbuilding on the Clyde (detail)
(Ministry of Information photo. Crown copyright reserved)

PLATE XXVI

Above:

GRAHAM SUTHERLAND. Devastation 1941

Below:

HENRY MOORE. Tube Shelter 1940

(Ministry of Information photos. Crown copyright reserved)

works of public service and not willing to spend their revenues in purchases of works of art. Indeed these organizations claimed the right to call the tune and not only not pay the piper but draw large revenues for themselves by charging a shilling or eighteen pence from every member of the public who attended the performance.

It is important to realize that these Academic organizations—which persist to-day—are self-elected bodies, priesthoods in service of themselves; and that in order to justify their existence they deem it necessary to propound artistic doctrine, to denounce all other forms of art as 'heresies', and to refuse to exhibit pictures by artists who question or defy their doctrines.

The doctrines of these Academic organizations have of necessity changed in the course of their history. But they have always been a canonization of some artistic 'heresy' of fifty years earlier; and the Academic organizations have always for this reason used the 'heresy' of fifty years earlier as a rod with which to chastise the dominant 'heresy' of their own day.

Thus in 1830 the French Academic doctrine, in defence of its members who were painting imitations of David's pictures, called the eighteenth-century art of David 'Real Art' and used it to chastise the Romantic 'heresy' of 1830; by 1880 the French

Academy had canonized the Romantic art of 1830 and were using it to chastise the Impressionist experiment of the 'seventies and 'eighties; and both the French and English Academic doctrines of 1930 have now canonized nineteenth-century Impressionism, which they refer to as 'Real Art', and use it to chastise the 'modern' or Cubist-classical movement. But the history of European art from 1880–1930 is the history of the original 'heresies', and the—quite literally—millions of works produced by Academicians and their followers in imitation of those 'heresies' fifty years later have no significance in art history at all.

At the turn of the nineteenth to the twentieth century, original artists tried to meet the obstructing Academic organizations by organizations of their own which would make their work known to the general public and bring some gate-money to their pockets on the Academic plan. In Paris, the Salon des Indépendants, the Salon d'Automne, the Salon des Tuileries, and so on, and in London the New English Art Club, the London Group, and so on, were successively created. But these counter-organizations soon showed a tendency to develop the vices of the Academic organizations and eventually most of the serious research artists evolved the system of the one-man show in a dealer's gallery, which is their usual method of making known their work in all capitals to-day.

As things stand at present there is now in all countries a definite cleavage between the Academic organizations and the experimenting research artists; the first still draw large revenues from the once-a-year-art-inspecting public (and, in England, also from letting their galleries for functions like the Flemish, Dutch, and Italian Exhibitions); and the second have now, everywhere, their own small public of dilettanti, collectors, critics, and enterprising dealers, whose support has enabled them to bring about the Cubist-Classical Renaissance of our time.

2

I have discussed the character of this contemporary Renaissance and its relation to nineteenth-century art in my book *The Modern Movement in Art* which was written to explain it.[1] Stated very briefly, it is a conscious attempt to defy the camera by the doctrine that architecture is the Mother of the Arts, an idea which starts with the assumption that painting and sculpture are fundamentally activities of the same kind as architecture; and at the same time it is a reaction in the field of thought against the Romantic Individualism of the nineteenth century, and a reaction in favour of an attitude to life that puts its faith more in order, intellect and collective effort than in the unfettered expression of individual emotion.

[1] *The Modern Movement in Art*, by R. H. Wilenski (Faber & Faber).

In France the nineteenth-century heralds of this
movement were Cézanne and Seurat who are related
to the Modern Movement (which has now spread to
most parts of the civilized world) in much the same
way that Michelangelo and Tintoretto were related
to the Baroque Movement of the seventeenth and
that Rembrandt was related to the Romantic Movement of the nineteenth century.

The pioneer work of Seurat and Cézanne has been
continued in the twentieth century by Pablo Picasso,
a young Spaniard domiciled in Paris who has been
the central figure of the Cubist-Classical movement
for the last twenty years. Picasso's early pictures
demonstrate that he had nineteenth-century Romantic art in his pocket. But he felt that the expression
of sensibility, and the cult of the emotive fragment,
were out of tune with the attitude of the new age; and
he laid the foundations of the new European art—
which is, incidentally, also the art of the New York
skyscraper—with those flat-pattern and box of bricks
non-representational pictures that have since become
famous. Later he built on that foundation in landscape, figure groups and portraits. As a Spaniard he
escaped the 1914—18 war and was able to continue
his experiments without interruption.

When the war came Picasso's attitude to art was
seen to be the only possible attitude to life itself in
the war conditions. The first shell blew nineteenth-

century Romantic Individualism to blazes. The cult
of individual sensibility and individual freedom was
clearly an obsolete ideal in this new phase of life.
Order, centralized control, co-operation, and disci-
pline became the new ideals; and Cubism became
the symbol of twentieth-century life.

3

In England, before the war, there was one artist,
Wyndham Lewis, who had seen the point of the
Cubist experiments in France; Lewis tried to explain
the Cubist attitude to young artists over here, and his
influence prepared them for their trials and triumphs
in the war.

All the young English artists of the Modern
Movement served in the war; and the war created
here a social organization which had need of art of
a certain character, and was willing to pay for it.

That organization was the Ministry of Information
which decided that records of the war on a large scale
might serve the political purpose of the moment and
also have historical importance. The Ministry accordingly secured power to transfer a number of
young artists from active service to its own ranks and
to employ them on painting pictures of the war.
Later, older artists who had not served were also
employed, and the Canadian War Memorials Committee commissioned a series of war pictures from

both types of artist for a War Memorial Hall in Ottawa.

The response of the younger artists to their opportunity was seen in one-man shows and large exhibitions organized by the Ministry and by the Canadian War Memorials Committee; and it can be seen to-day to some extent in the Imperial War Museum and the Canadian Galleries. Lewis painted gunners in the field; Paul Nash painted comments on the devastated areas; C. R. W. Nevinson painted soldiers on the march and men in hospitals; W. Roberts painted a gas attack; Stanley Spencer mule convoys bearing wounded in Macedonia; and Eric Kennington, in a picture called 'The Victims', showed Canadian soldiers marching through mountains of rusty scrap iron and barbed wire. These young artists, who had seen modern war from the inside, were yet able to grasp its configuration as a whole and to set that down in the pictorial language of their day because already, before the war, they had begun to look on the Cubist attitude as the symbol of twentieth-century life. The older artists painted the twentieth-century war in the romantic spirit of the nineteenth century.

4

After the war both the French and English artists of the Modern Movement returned to their quasi-scientific labours of research; and such artists are now to be found in all civilized lands. Artists of this calibre know that their researches are an aspect of the intellectual effort of the age; they know that they can expect neither moral encouragement nor pecuniary support from the Academic organizations; and they know that their work, like that of the research scientists, must of necessity be incomprehensible to the general public till some popular artists have exploited it in social forms.

Such exploitation now takes place on every side. We see the results of the Cubist-Classical researches in architecture, in sculpture, and in furniture; we see them in painting all over the world and especially in Italy where the classical tree has so frequently borne fruit; we see them in the streamlines of motor-cars, in the new arterial roads, in clothes, in textiles, in publicity drawings and the covers of magazines.

In spite of protests from old gentlemen, who still live mentally in the Romantic nineteenth century, formal order and formal design are gradually replacing expressions of personal emotion and records of emotive fragments in all fields of art. Gradually, all the world is beginning to realize that we live in an age of co-ordinated effort, of instantaneous world-wide communications, of moving photographs and aeroplanes, of skyscrapers, of steel and concrete factories, and scientific skill; that this age has a pattern of its own as all ages have had before it; and that the Cubist artists, who were ridiculed and reviled, were the first to recognize this pattern, to accept it, and to resolve to work out its development.

5

Thus the human activity that we call art, which began with the creation of the magic image to secure some vital need, which has been at other times a most powerful instrument of tyranny and at others again a most powerful instrument of religion, has now become an activity pursued for its own sake by a small group of experimenting artists, who are kept going by another small group consisting partly of people who believe in the metaphysical value of this work as an accompaniment and symbol of contemporary thought, and partly of people who hope to make profit eventually from these artists' researches.

Socialism or another war may make it impossible for the experimenting artists and their supporters to exist. But after both groups have disappeared, Socialism, or another Ministry of Information, may one day decide to use art as an instrument for imposing its ideas on the people as a whole as Pharaohs and Caesars and the Church have so often used it in the past. If that happens will the artists be forthcoming? Undoubtedly—since demand creates supply.

PLATE XXVII

LEON UNDERWOOD. Rhythm of Life

(*Lino Engraving*)

PLATE XXVIII

PICASSO.   Mother and Child
(*Photo.   Author's collection*)

EPILOGUE (1945)

I

SINCE I wrote the last section of my outline, in 1930, events have shown artists that an understanding of the mutual relations between civilization and culture is of first importance for their survival in the modern world. The words civilization and culture are commonly used in a number of senses. But if the following meanings are accepted the problem, I think, stands clear.

Civilization, I submit, is local and temporary government concerned with local and temporary social services; it is local organization of local security, health and satisfactions; it is not a condition of grace or disgrace or any other type of condition, but a type of action performed by local temporary governors (civilizers) on the governed (civilizees) within their orbit at the moment. So far all attempts to create a single universal civilization have failed; there have always been and there still are a number of different civilizations operating in different places at the same time; these civilizations are of different levels—a civilization being good in the degree in which it is genuinely concerned with promoting the interests of the civilizees and bad in the degree in which it is concerned with promoting its own interests, i.e. the interests of the governors. Quarrels between civilizations of different levels can easily cause wars.

Culture, I submit, is also not a condition of grace or disgrace or any other type of condition (it is not, for example, the condition of being 'educated' in any particular way or to any particular level). Like civilization it is a form of action. For action to be culture it must be creative action which enlarges human experience of life as such; and the degree of its goodness is not dependent like the goodness of civilization on the degree of its direct service to local and temporary conditions, but on the degree of its enlargement of experience. This type of action is pursued by research scientists and original artists. There is no difference between art and science on this plane. Science is good if it contributes to the enlargement of science; art is good if it contributes to the enlargement of art. Culture's business ends when it has put its contributions on the table. What happens then depends on the local civilization, which may suppress it, or use it locally, or allow its publication to the world.

In Britain, the central type of Western European democracy, the normal relation between culture and the local civilization works out something like this: The governing civilizers say to culture: 'We will protect you against brutal louts at home and abroad; we will guarantee you absolute freedom in research and absolute freedom in the publication of the results (provided that they contain nothing libellous, blasphemous or obscene and even then we will look the other way unless our hand is forced by circumstances); in return we reserve the right to use your discoveries in any way which may seem good to us; and when you die we will see to it that you get a half column in *The Times*.' That is a reasonably fair bargain on both sides. But when the local civilizers receive the contributions made by culture they often do not know what to do with them because they do not understand them, and they are well aware that most of the local civilizees will understand them even less. They therefore call for an intermediate type of action—the action of the cultural vulgarizer, whose task it is to bridge the gap between culture's action on the one hand and civilization's requirements on the other. To these cultural vulgarizers the civilizers say: 'You see this formula by this research chemist; put it into words which the man in the street can understand and let us know whether it can help us to make a cheaper fountain pen or a more devastating explosive or anything else practical and useful.' Or they say: 'You see this architect's plan for a city with no ground floors and no streets; do something to it to make it look more normal so that we can use it for our new Civic Centre; we must move with the times, you know, our civilizees expect it; but we must have *some* ground floors and *some* streets'. Or they say, this time to the Royal Academy: 'You see this odd-looking picture which represents nothing recognizable. Our civilizees are asking for modern art and we want to give it them—within reason. Please do something on these lines but less extreme.' The cultural vulgarizers, though immensely useful to civilizers, seem of course to culture the devil incarnate. But since the men of culture are not concerned with the local use of their contributions and are, or should be, by the time the vulgarizers appear, already engaged in making further contributions, they cannot logically complain.

2

Those conditions are normal in modern democratic states. But the 1914–18 war imposed for the time and of necessity a more authoritarian pattern on modern civilizations, a pattern which the Cubist artists had already unconsciously symbolized in the pre-war years; and in the emergency the men of culture left their studios and laboratories to offer direct service to their local civilizers. Much the same thing has happened again in the present war; culture, recognizing that the security and freedom which a liberal civilization provides for it depend on the security of the civilization itself, has again offered local temporary service; and as far as art in Britain is concerned, civilization (in the persons of the Ministry of Information and Sir Kenneth Clark, Director of the National Gallery) has accepted that offer and even found ways and means of allowing culture to pursue to some extent and at intervals its own true non-local and non-temporary work as well.

But before these lines are printed or soon after, the present war may be ended, and a new generation of young artists may be starting their careers. These young people will need the normal conditions of a modern democratic state—the conditions which last prevailed in the nineteen-twenties. In that decade original artists and intellectuals of all kinds, relieved for a space from the deadening fear of German aggression, plunged healthily into critical surveys and creative experiments and transformed the Cubist pattern of the 1914–18 war years to the Associationist pattern which I have described elsewhere.[1] The achievements of the nineteen-twenties in art and science were, in fact, immense; and it is essential to remember this because from early in the nineteen-thirties the forces which were about to inflict the old tortures of the Inquisition in Gestapo prisons and which were about to help General Franco to invade Spain, began a world campaign of propaganda against the normal conditions of democracy and tried to represent the abnormal authoritarian con-

1 See my *Modern French Painters* (Faber).

G

ditions which can only be justified by war emergencies, as justifiable, normal and desirable in peace. These authoritarian forces were out to make impossible free associationist contacts, free criticism of authority, free reading, free thought and free publication of original contributions in science and art. For this purpose the previous decade, in which these freedoms were widely found, was dubbed the 'Cocktail Twenties' by this propaganda and all its characters were shamelessly denigrated. This propaganda was especially directed against the young who aspired to make personal contributions. It was indeed the tragedy of the nineteen-thirties that the young people were continuously, as the phrase goes, being 'got at'; they were not given a square deal in the idealistic years of adolescence; they were not told facts, but bullied into adopting beliefs which placed them in the power of the propagandists; they were not helped, they were exploited. 'We, civilization, are infallible', the propagandists said to them, 'serve us without question and then you can hold your head up as a useful member of society; if you ask questions or try to make your own contribution you are a pretentious nuisance and we will wipe you out.' Reduced to perplexed humility by this onslaught and wishing to escape from it, many young artists in the nineteen-thirties sought refuge in the communist doctrines—only to find there an ideology, at that time at any rate, as authoritarian as the other; and it was only the exceptional young person who saw then that normal and tolerable conditions were in fact those which had prevailed in the previous decade so incessantly sneered at and maligned.

Civilizers in the coming post-war years will once again call for service from artists and once again they will get it—direct service from cultural vulgarizers and indirect service from culture. That will be no tragedy provided the civilizers accept the precepts that though culture may, and indeed should, offer direct service to local civilization in war emergencies, it must never be asked for such service in the normal conditions of a modern liberal society and never, even in wartime, be browbeaten to silence or forced to say what the civilizers wish. All civilizations get the culture they deserve; and in the modern world the only civilizers who can get from the men of culture the best they can give, are those willing to provide them with security and then leave them to contribute what they please. In such conditions the young artists are left free to act as cultural vulgarizers if they want to and also free to act as culture if they have the necessary gifts and grit.

INDEX OF PAINTERS, SCULPTORS, AND ARCHITECTS

mentioned in text with their dates

PRINTED IN
GREAT BRITAIN
BY THE
BOWERING PRESS
PLYMOUTH